JESUS

For God so loved the world, that he gave his only begotten Son, that whosoever believeth in him should not perish, but have everlasting life.
John 3:16

FREDERICK L. BURWELL

XULON PRESS

Xulon Press
2301 Lucien Way #415
Maitland, FL 32751
407.339.4217
www.xulonpress.com

© 2022 by Frederick L. Burwell

All rights reserved solely by the author. The author guarantees all contents are original and do not infringe upon the legal rights of any other person or work. No part of this book may be reproduced in any form without the permission of the author.

Due to the changing nature of the Internet, if there are any web addresses, links, or URLs included in this manuscript, these may have been altered and may no longer be accessible. The views and opinions shared in this book belong solely to the author and do not necessarily reflect those of the publisher. The publisher therefore disclaims responsibility for the views or opinions expressed within the work.

Unless otherwise indicated, Scripture quotations taken from the Holy Bible, New Living Translation (NLT). Copyright ©1996, 2004, 2007 by Tyndale House Foundation. Used by permission of Tyndale House Publishers, Inc.

Paperback ISBN-13: 978-1-6628-5251-0
Ebook ISBN-13: 978-1-6628-5252-7

Author's Note

We all know that this world is fast-paced, and full of technology. It is continuously moving forward, and there is no turning back. Stop and take a look around. How often does family get together and reminisce about the good ol' days? Not too many huh, especially with COVID-19 running rampant. Nowadays, families only come together for two occasions: weddings and funerals. Sad to say but mostly funerals. Most of the time family stays will be brief. What has happened to big mama's house? Remember when the whole family met and talked over that enormous meal? In the world we live in, most families are scattered about the earth like grass seeds.

My intention was to create a short book for young and old to inspire and remind us all how much we need God in our lives. Let's get back to the Bible and get a closer relationship with our Lord and Savior Jesus Christ. Hopefully, people from all walks of life will read this book and be touched. If you have not accepted Jesus Christ as your personal Savior, do it today. Time is running out; don't get left behind. Thank you all so much and may God bless you!

Acknowledgements

Lord, into your hands I place this day, all that I have and do and say', Oh, grant that every hour be filled with thoughts, and actions you have willed.

> To break sin's grip,
> put yourself in God's hands.

3 Things You Must Do

Pray: You talk to God
Read your Bible: God talks to you
Witness: You talk for God

Foreword

First, and foremost I want to thank my Lord, and Savior Jesus Christ. This book was written through the inspiration of Scripture. All scripture is given by inspiration from God, and is profitable for doctrine, reproof, correction, and instruction in righteousness. Second Timothy 3:16 states, May God receive all the Glory. I would like to dedicate this book to my deceased family members, Ressie and Susie Woodard (my grandparents), Calvin B. Currin (my stepfather), Spencer and Beatrice Currin (my grandparents), Faye Woodard (my aunt), Robin Woodard (my aunt), Carolyn Tobey (my aunt), and Elaine Woodard (my aunt). Rest in peace family. I'm sorry for not adding any other family members who have gone on to glory, but I wanted to recognize my immediate family who raised me from a little boy and guided me to become the God-fearing man I am today. I salute you. Gone but never forgotten. I pray that the Lord will bless this, and someone somewhere will be touched, no matter what it is they are going through. Whenever you think you got it bad, Just remember Jesus had it ten times worse, and he committed no sin.

Enjoy,
Frederick L. Burwell

Creation
Genesis 1:1–2:7

Genesis 1:1 states, "In the beginning God created the heavens and the earth."

Genesis 2:7 states, "And the Lord God formed a man's body from the dust of the ground and breathed into it the breath of life."

A Perfect Creator

Doesn't God deserve all the glory? Who is more perfect than him? Why, in this day and time, are there still people who do not believe in God? It is written that God created the heavens and the earth, and formed man's body from dust. How much plainer can it get? All God's creation!

Day One: Light (day) and darkness (night)
Day Two: Firmament (Heaven)
Day Three: The Earth, seas, grass, and fruit
Day Four: The sun, moon, and stars
Day Five: The fish and birds
Day Six: Cattle, beasts, creeping things, and man and woman
Day Seven: God rested (the holy day)

Our God is perfect who else could do this? Do you know of another person greater than my God?

Passover 2022 will begin on the evening of Friday, April 15.
It ends the evening of Saturday, April 23.

PASSOVER
Exodus 12

Exodus 12:23 states:

> For the Lord will pass through the land and strike down the Egyptians. But when he sees the blood on the top and sides of the doorframe, the Lord will pass over your home. He will not permit the Destroyer to enter and strike down your first born.

God's Instructions

You must read the whole chapter of Exodus 12 to see the power of God. This was God's last plague that freed his people from Pharaoh. Whenever God makes a promise, he delivers. God instructed Moses and Aaron to announce to the whole community that on the tenth day of the month each family had to choose a lamb or young goat as sacrifice. The animal had to be a one-year-old male with no physical defects. They were told to slaughter the animal then roast and eat it. Also, they had to take some of lamb's blood and smear it on the top and sides of the doorframe of the house where the lamb was eaten. The Lord said on that night He would pass through the land of Egypt and kill all the firstborn sons and firstborn male animals in the land of Egypt. The blood you have smeared on your doorposts will serve as a sign. When I see the blood I will pass over you. Death will not touch you when I strike the land of Egypt. They were covered by the blood, doesn't that sound familiar? Jesus died on the cross and shed his precious blood so that we may have eternal life. Thank God for his grace and mercy and that we are covered by the blood of Jesus.

The Ten Commandments

Exodus 20:1–2 states, "And God instructed the people as follows: I am the Lord your God, who rescued you from slavery in Egypt."

God Gives Moses the Ten Commandments

In Exodus 20 God gave Moses the Ten Commandments, which we should all be following. Let's look at them.

- Do not worship any other gods besides me.
- Do not make idols of any kind, whether in the shape of birds or animals or fish.
- Do not misuse the name of the Lord your God. The Lord will not let you go unpunished if you misuse his name.
- Remember to observe the Sabbath day by keeping it holy. Six days of the week are set apart for work and on seventh day you must rest.
- Honor your father and mother. Then you will live a long, full life in the land. God will give you.
- Do not murder.
- Do not commit adultery.
- Do not steal.
- Do not testify falsely against your neighbor.
- Do not covet your neighbor's house. Do not covet your neighbor's wife, male or female servant, ox or donkey, or anything else your neighbor owns.

What does covet mean? Covet means to eagerly desire something that someone else has. The people heard thunder, and a loud blast of the horn, they also saw lightning, and some billowing from the mountain. They all stood at a distance, trembling with fear. They were so scared they told Moses to tell them what God said because they felt if God spoke directly to them that they would die. Moses told them not to be afraid when God showed his awesome power, and from then on let their fear of him keep them from sinning.

God's Love
Psalm 23

Psalm 23 was written around 1000 BC attributed to King David.

God always protects and provides.

A psalm of David

> The Lord is my shepherd; I have everything I need. He lets me rest in green meadows. he leads me beside peaceful streams. He renews my strength. He guides me along right paths bringing honor to his name. Even when I walk through the dark valley of death I will not be afraid for you are close beside me. your rod and your staff protect and comfort me. You prepare a feast for me in the presence of my enemies. you welcome me as a guest, anointing my head with oil. My cup overflows with blessings, Surely your goodness and unfailing love will pursue me all the days of my life, and I will live in the house of the Lord forever.

This is a very popular scripture that billions are familiar with. Most of the time it is read when walking a body to the grave at funerals, but the true meaning has nothing to do with that corpse. The Lord is our guide and we are the sheep. God makes us lay down in green pastures, where there is plenty to eat. Beware of wolves, which are false prophets which were never called by God, but took it upon themselves to become messengers of God. Even though at some point we will have troubled waters; God leads us to peaceful waters. Only God can calm those troubled waters through his word. Peace be still. God gives us restoration by restoring our soul when we feel like we're falling apart. Instead of a burial, this scripture deals with a state of being a person who diligently seeks God. At a person's lowest point. I walk through the valley of the shadow of death, I will fear no evil because God gives me green pastures which is his external word.

Forgiveness
Psalm 51

This is a psalm from David regarding the time Nathan, the prophet, came to him after David had committed adultery with Bathsheba.

A Request for God's Forgiveness

Have mercy on me, O God, because of your unfailing love. Because of your great compassion, blot out the stain of my sins. Wash me clean from my guilt. Purify me from my sin. For I recognize my shameful deeds – they haunt me day and night. Against you, and you alone, have I sinned; I have done what is evil in your sight. You will be proved right in what you say, and your Judgement against me is Just. For I was born a sinner – yes, from the moment my mother conceived me. But you desire honesty from the heart, so you can teach me to be wise in my inmost being. Purify me from my sins, and I will be clean; wash me, and I will be whiter than snow. Oh, give me back my Joy again; you have broken me – now let me rejoice. Don't keep looking at my sins. Remove the stain of my guilt. Create in me a clean heart, O God. Renew a right spirit within me. Do not banish me from your presence, and don't take your Holy Spirit from me. Restore to me again the Joy of your Salvation, and make me willing to obey you. Then I will teach your ways to sinners, and they will return to you. Forgive me for shedding blood, O God who saves then I will Joyfully sing of your forgiveness. Unseal my lips O Lord, that I may praise you. you would not be pleased with sacrifices, or I would bring them. If I brought you a burnt offering, you would not accept it. The sacrifice you want is a broken spirit. A broken and repentant heart. O God, you will not despise. Look with favor on Zion and help her; rebuild the walls of Jerusalem. Then you will be pleased with worthy sacrifices and with our whole burnt offerings; and bulls will again be sacrificed on your altar.

GOD'S LAWS
Psalm 119

Psalm 119

The longest Psalm in the Bible is Psalm 119. It is 176 verses in length because of its poetic structure as an acrostic of every letter of the Hebrew alphabet. The length is appropriate for this Psalm's theme of devotion to God and His word. It is also the longest chapter in the Bible.

Your Word is a Lamp for My Feet and a Light for My Path

Happy are people of integrity, who follow the law of the Lord. Happy are those who obey his decrees and search for him with all their hearts. They do not compromise with evil, and they walk only in his paths. You have charged us to keep your commandments carefully. Oh, that my actions would consistently reflect your principles. Please don't give up on me! How can a young person stay pure? By obeying your word and following its rules. I have tried my best to find you – don't let me wander from your commands. I have hidden your word in my heart, that I might not sin against you. Blessed are you, O Lord; teach me your principles. I have recited aloud all the laws you have given us. I have rejoiced in your decrees as much as in riches. I will study your commandments and reflect on your ways. I will delight in your principles and not forget your word. Be good to your Servant, that I may live and obey your word. Open my eyes to see the wonderful truths in your law. I am but a foreigner here on earth, I need the guidance of your commands. Don't hide them from me! I am overwhelmed continually with a desire for your laws. You rebuke those cursed proud ones who wander from your commands. Don't let them scorn and insult me, for I have obeyed your decrees. Even princes sit and speak against me but I will meditate on your principles.

Your decrees please me; they give me wise advice. I lie in the dust, completely discouraged; revive me by your word. I told you my plans, and you answered. Now teach me your principles. Help me understand the meaning of your commandments, and I will meditate on your wonderful miracles. I weep with grief; encourage me by your word. Keep me from lying to myself, give me the privilege of knowing your law. I have chosen to be faithful, I have determined to live by your laws. I cling to your decrees. Lord, don't let me be put to shame! If you will help me, I will run to follow your commands.

Teach me, O Lord, to follow every one of your principles. Give me understanding and I will obey your law. I will put it into practice with all my heart. Make me walk along the path of your commands, for that is where my happiness is found. Give me an eagerness for your decrees; do not inflict me with love for money! Turn my eyes from worthless things and give me life through your word. Reassure me of your promise, which is for these who honor you. Help me abandon my shameful ways; your laws are all I want in life. I long to obey your commandments! Renew my life with your goodness.

Lord, give to me your unfailing love, the salvation that you promised me. Then I will have an answer for those who taunt me, for I trust in your word. Do not scratch your word of truth from me, for my only hope is in your laws. I will keep on obeying your law forever and forever. I will walk in freedom, for I have devoted myself to your commandments. I will speak to Kings about your decrees, and I will not be ashamed. How I delight in your commands! How I love them! I honor and love your commands. I meditate on your principles.

Remember your promise to me, for it is my only hope. Your promise revives me; it comforts me in all my troubles. The proud hold in me utter contempt, but I do not turn away from your law. I meditate on your age – old laws; O Lord, they comfort me. I am furious with the wicked, those who reject your law. Your principles have been the music of my life throughout the years of my pilgrimage. I reflect at night on who you are, O Lord, and

I obey your law because of this. This is my happy way of life: obeying your commandments.

Lord, you are mine! I promise to obey your words! With all my heart I want your blessings. Be merciful just as you promised. I promised the direction of my life, and I turned to follow your statutes. I will hurry, without lingering, to obey your commands. Evil people try to drag me into sin, but I am firmly anchored to your law. At midnight I rise to thank you for your just laws. Anyone who fears you is my friend – anyone who obeys your commandments O Lord, the earth is full of unfailing love; teach me your principles.

You have done many good things for me, Lord, just as you promised. I believe in your commands; now teach me good judgement and knowledge. I used to wander off until you disciplined me; but now I closely follow your word. You are good and do only good; teach me your principles. Arrogant people have made up lies about me, but in truth I obey your commandments with all my heart. Their hearts are dull and stupid, but I delight in your law. The suffering you sent was good for me, for it taught me to pay attention to your principles. Your law is more valuable to me than millions in gold and silver.

You made me; you created me. Now give me the sense to follow your commands. May all who fear you find in me a cause for joy, for I have put my hope in your word. I know, O Lord, that your decisions are fair; you disciplined me because I needed it. Now let your unfailing love comfort me, just as you promised me, your servant.

Surround me with your tender mercies so I may live, for your law is my delight. Bring disgrace upon the arrogant people who lied about me; meanwhile, I will concentrate on your commandments. Let me be reconciled with all who fear you and know your decrees. May I be blameless in keeping your principles; then I will never have to be ashamed.

I faint with longing for your salvation; but I have put my hope in your word. My eyes are straining to see your promises come true. When will you comfort me? I am shriveled like a wineskin in the smoke, exhausted with waiting. But I cling to your principles and obey them, how long must I wait? When will you punish those who persecute me? These arrogant people who hate your law have dug deep pits for me to fall into. All your commands are trustworthy. Protect me from those who hunt me down without cause. They almost finished me off, but I refused to abandon your commandments. In your unfailing love spare my life; then I can continue to obey your decrees.

Forever, O Lord, your word stands firm in heaven. Your faithfulness extends to every generation as enduring as the earth you created. Your laws remain true today, for everything serves your plans. If your law hadn't sustained me with Joy, I would have died in my misery. I will never forget your commandments, for you have used them to restore my Joy and health, I am yours; save me! For I have applied myself to obey your commandments. Though the wicked hide along the way to kill me, I will quietly keep my mind on your decrees. Even perfection has its limits, but your commands have no limit.

Oh, how I love your law! I think about it all day long. Your commands make me wiser than my enemies, for your commands are my constant guide. Yes, I have more insight than my teachers for I am always thinking of your decrees. I am even wiser than my elders, for I have kept your commandments. I have refused to walk on any path of evil, that I may remain obedient to your word. I haven't turned away from your laws, for you have taught me well. How sweet are your words to my taste; they are sweeter than honey. Your commandments give me understanding; no wonder I hate every false way of life.

Your word is a lamp for my feet and a light for my path. I've promised it once, and I'll promise again: I will obey your wonderful laws. I have suffered much, O Lord, restore my life again, just as you promised. Lord accept my grateful thanks and teach me your laws. My life constantly hangs in the balance, but I will not stop obeying your law. The wicked have set their traps for me along your path, but I will not turn from your commandments.

Your decrees are my treasure; they are truly my heart's delight. I am determined to keep your principles, even forever, to the very end.

I hate those who are undecided about you, but my choice is clear – I love your law. You are my refuge and my shield; your word is my only source of hope. Get out of my life, you evil-minded people, for I intend to obey the commands of my God. Lord, sustain me as you promised that I may live! Do not let my hope be crushed. Sustain me and I will be saved; then I will meditate on your principles continually. But you have rejected all who stray from your principles, they are only fooling themselves. All the wicked of the earth are the scum to you skim off; no wonder I love to obey your decrees! I tremble in fear of you; I fear your judgements.

Don't leave me to the mercy of my enemies, for I have done what is just and right. Please guarantee a blessing for me. Don't let those who are arrogant oppress me! My eyes strain to see your deliverance, to see the truth of your promise fulfilled. I am your servant; deal with me in unfailing love, and teach me your principles. Give discernment to me, your servant; then I will understand your decrees. Lord, it is time for you to act, for these evil people have broken your law. Truly, I love your commands more than gold, even the finest gold. Truly, each of your commandments is right, that is why I hate every false way.

Your decrees are wonderful. No wonder I obey them! As your words are taught, they give light; even the simple can understand them. I open my mouth, panting expectantly, longing for your commands. Come and show me your mercy, as you do for all who love your name. Guide my steps by your word, so I will not be overcome by any evil. Rescue me from the oppression of evil people; then I can obey your commandments. Look down on me with love; teach me all your principles. Rivers of tears gush from my eyes because people disobey your law.

O Lord, you are righteous, and your decisions are fair. Your decrees are perfect; they are entirely worthy of our trust. I am overwhelmed with rage, for my enemies have disregarded your words. Your promises have been thoroughly tested; that is why I love them so much. I am insignificant and despised, but I don't forget your commandments. Your justice is eternal, and your law is perfectly true. As pressure and stress bear down on me, I find joy in your commands, your decrees are always fair; help me to understand them, that I may live.

I pray with all my heart; answer me, Lord! I will obey your principles. I cry out to you; save me, that I may obey your decrees. I rise early, before the sun is up; I cry out for help and put my hope in your words. I stay awake through the night, thinking about your promise. In your faithful love, O Lord, hear my cry; in your justice, save my life. Those lawless people are coming near to attack me; they live far from your law. But you are near, O Lord, and all your commands are true, I have known from my earliest days that your decrees never change.

Look down upon my sorrows and rescue me, for I have not forgotten your law. Argue my case; take my side! Protect my life as you promised. The wicked are far from salvation, for they do not bother with your principles. Lord, how great is your mercy, in your justice, give me back my life. Many persecute and trouble me, yet I have not swerved from your decrees. I hate these traitors because they care nothing for your word. See how I love your commandments, Lord. Give back my life because of your unfailing love. All your words are true; all your just laws will stand forever.

Powerful people harass me without cause but my heart trembles only at your word. I rejoice in your word like one who finds a great treasure. I hate and abhor all falsehood, but I love your law. I will praise you seven times a day because all your laws are Just. Those who love your law have great peace and do not stumble. I long for your salvation, Lord, so I have obeyed your commands. I have obeyed your decrees, and I love them very much. Yes, I obey your commandments and decrees because you know everything I do.

O Lord listen to my cry; give me the discerning mind you promised. Listen to my prayer; rescue me as you promised. Let my lips burst forth with praise, for you have taught me your principles. Let my tongue sing about your word, for all your commands are right. Stand ready to help me, for I have chosen to follow your commandments. O Lord, I have longed for your salvation, and your law is my delight. Let me live so I can praise you, and may your laws sustain me: I have wandered away like a lost sheep; come and find me, for I have not forgotten your commands.

God's Knowledge
PSALM 139

Psalm 139

This passage speaks of the faithfulness of God to me every time. God will never let me go. I am His, and that knowledge humbles me and keeps me in His love. Read this Psalm slowly and let the Lord speak to you today.

The Lord Knows Everything

O Lord, you have examined my heart and know everything about me. You know when I sit down or stand up. You know my every thought when far away. You chart the path ahead of me and tell me where to stop and rest. Every moment you know where I am. You know what I am going to say even before I say it, Lord. You both precede and follow me. You place your hand of blessing on my head. Such knowledge is too wonderful for me, too great for me to know!

I can never escape from your spirit! I can never get away from your presence! If I go up to heaven, you are there; if I go down to the place of the dead, you are there. If I ride the wings of the morning, if I dwell by the farthest oceans, even there your hand will guide me, and your strength will support me. I could ask the darkness to hide me and the light around me to become night – but even in darkness I cannot hide from you. To you the night shines as bright as day. Darkness and light are both alike to you.

You made all the delicate, inner parts of my body and knit me together in my mother's womb. Thank you for making me so wonderfully complex! Your workmanship is marvelous – and how well I know it. You watched me as I was being formed in utter seclusion, as I was woven together in the dark of the womb. You saw me before I was born. Every day of my life was recorded in your book. Every moment was laid out before a single day had passed.

How precious are your thoughts about me, O God! They are innumerable! I can't even count them; they outnumber the grains of sand! And when I wake up in the morning, you are still with me!

O God, if only you would destroy the wicked. Get out of my life, you murderers! They blaspheme you; your enemies take your name in vain! O Lord, Shouldn't I hate those who hate you? Shouldn't I despise those who resist you? Yes, I hate them with complete hatred for your enemies are my enemies. Search me, O God, and know my heart; test me and know my thoughts. Point out anything in me that offends you and lead me along the path of everlasting life.

WISDOM
Proverbs 1–2

Proverbs 1–2

The book of Proverbs contains practical instructions for successful living. It teaches that there is special wisdom revealed by God as well as innate wisdom or common sense, and both must play a part in daily life. This book is a collection of practical wisdom from many centuries, and it deals with Such diverse matters as the discipline for children, social justice, foolish talk, and money. It ends by describing the character of an outstanding wife. Since it's almost 2023, and with the pandemic, climate change, murders, and everything else, our people need wisdom right now, and knowledge begins with fear of the Lord. This is what is written about wisdom.

The Purpose of Proverbs

These are the proverbs of Solomon, David's son, King of Israel. The purpose of these proverbs is to teach people wisdom and discipline, and to help them understand wise sayings. Through these proverbs will make the simple-minded clever. They will give knowledge and purpose to young people.

Let those who are wise listen to these proverbs and become even wiser.

And let those who understand receive guidance by exploring the depth of meaning in these proverbs, parables, wise sayings, and riddles. Fear of the Lord is the beginning of knowledge. Only fools despise wisdom and discipline.

A Father's Exhortation: Acquire Wisdom

Listen, my child, to what your father teaches you. Don't neglect your mother's teaching. What you learn from them will crown you with grace and clothe you with honor. My child, if sinners entice you, turn your back on them! They may say, "come and join us. Let's hide and kill someone! Let's ambush the innocent! Let's swallow them alive as the grave swallows its victims. Though they are in the prime of life, they will go down into the pit of death. And the loot we'll get! We'll fill our houses with all kinds of things! Come on, throw in your lot with us; We'll split our loot with you."

Don't go along with them, my child! Stay far away from their paths, they rush to commit crimes. They hurry to commit murder. When a bird sees a trap being set, it stays away. But not these people! They set an ambush for themselves; they booby-trap their own lives! Such is the fate of all who are greedy for gain. It ends up robbing them of life.

Wisdom shouts in the Streets

Wisdom shouts in the streets. She cries out in the public square. She calls out to the crowds along the main street, and to those in front of city hall. "You simpletons!" she cries. How long will you go on being simpleminded? How long will you mockers relish your mocking? How long will you fools fight the facts? Come here and listen to me! I'll pour out the spirit of wisdom upon you and make you wise.

I called you so often, but you didn't come. I reached out to you, but you paid no attention. You ignored my advice and rejected the correction I offered. So, I will laugh when you are in trouble! I will mock you when disaster overtakes you – when calamity overcomes you like a storm, when you are engulfed by trouble and when anguish and distress overwhelm you.

"I will not answer when they cry for help. Even though they anxiously search for me, they will not find me. For they hated knowledge and chose not to fear the Lord. They rejected my advice and paid no attention when I corrected them. That is why they must eat the bitter fruit of living their own way. They must experience the full terror of the path they have chosen. For they are simpletons who turn away from me – to death. They are fools, and their own complacency will destroy them.

But all who listen to me will live in peace and safety, unafraid of harm."

The Benefits of Wisdom

My child, listen to me and treasure my instructions. Tune your ears to wisdom and concentrate on understanding. Cry out for insight and understanding. Search for them as you would for lost money or hidden treasure. Then you will understand what it means to fear the Lord, and you will gain knowledge of God. For the Lord grants wisdom! From his mouth come knowledge and understanding. He grants a treasure of good sense to the godly. He is their shield, protecting those who walk with integrity. He guards the paths of Justice and protects those who are faithful to him.

Then you will understand what is right, just, and fair, and you will know how to find the right course of action every time. For wisdom will enter your heart, and knowledge will fill you with joy. Wise planning will watch over you. Understanding will keep you safe.

Wisdom will save you from evil people, from those whose speech is corrupt. These people turn from right ways to walk down dark and evil paths. They rejoice in doing wrong, and they enjoy evil as it turns things upside down. What they do is crooked, and their ways are wrong.

Wisdom will save you from the immoral woman, from the flattery of the adulterous woman. She has abandoned her husband and ignores the covenant she made before God. Entering her house leads to death; it is the road to hell. The man who visits her is doomed. He will never reach the paths of life.

Follow the steps of good men instead and stay on the paths of the righteous. For only the upright will live in the land, and those who have integrity will remain in it. But the wicked will be removed from the land, and the treacherous will be destroyed.

People it's time to wake up. It's time to turn to God and follow his commandments. If you were to die right now; where would you go? Wouldn't you like to know for sure that Heaven would be your home? You can't go around thinking you are holy and sanctified living your life the way you want. We belong to Jesus. Jesus paid the ultimate price on the cross for the whole world, yet we still reject him, and choose not to follow his commandments. God is displaying all the signs that his return is near, so I suggest we turn to God today, and pray for some wisdom and understanding.

A Good Wife
PROVERBS 31:10-30

Proverbs 31

The Bible, in Proverbs 31, defines a virtuous woman as one who leads her home with integrity, discipline, and more. All the virtues she practices are aimed at making her husband's life better, teaching her children, and serving God. This essentially, is the meaning of a virtuous woman.

A Wife of Noble Character

First, the definition of noble is someone who has high morals and ideals or people who are royalty or who have good breeding. An example of noble is a person who is always honest and charitable. Having or showing high moral qualities or ideals, or greatness of character; lofty.

Who can find a virtuous and capable wife? She is worth more than precious rubies. Her husband can trust her, and she will greatly enrich his life. She will not hinder him but help him all her life.

She finds wool and flax and busily spins it. She is like a merchant's ship; she brings her food from afar. She gets up before dawn to prepare breakfast for her household and plan the day's work for her servant girls. She goes out to inspect a field and buys it; with her earnings she plants a vineyard.

She is energetic and strong, a hard worker. She watches for bargains; her lights burn late into the night. Her hands are busy spinning thread, her fingers twisting fiber.

She extends a helping hand to the poor and opens her arms to the needy. She has no fear of winter for her household because all of them have warm clothes. She quilts her own bedspreads. She dresses like royalty in gowns of finest cloth.

Her husband is well known, for he sits in the council meeting with the other civic leaders.

She makes belted linen garments and sashes to sell to the merchants. She is clothed with strength and dignity, and she laughs with no fear of the future. When she speaks, her words are wise, and kindness is the rule when she gives instructions. She carefully watches all that goes on in her household and does not have to bear the consequences of laziness.

Her children stand and bless her. Her husband praises her. "There are many virtuous and capable women in the world, but you surpass them all!"

Charm is deceptive, and beauty does not last; but a woman who fears the Lord will be greatly praised.

These days, a good woman is hard to find, but I believe you just have to ask God to bring the right person into your life and have a little patience. It will happen unexpectedly— sooner than you think. He did it for me. If it's in the Lord's will, March 2022 will be twenty years for me. I look back at my life and see how God has truly blessed me.

A Time for Everything
Ecclesiastes 3

Ecclesiastes 3

Ecclesiastes 3:1–8 is a well-known passage that deals with the balanced, cyclical nature of life and says that there is a proper time for everything. There is a time for everything, and a season for every activity under the heavens.

Everything Has Got Its Own Time

There is a time for everything, a season for every activity under heaven. A time to be born and a time to die. A time to plant and a time to harvest. A time to kill and a time to heal. (Killing is in reference to the Old Testament where God, Himself, sanctioned or ended human lives.) A time to tear down and a time to rebuild. A time to cry and a time to laugh. A time to grieve and a time to dance. A time to scatter stones and a time to gather stones. A time to embrace and a time to turn away. A time to search and a time to lose. A time to keep and a time to throw away. A time to tear and a time to mend. A time to be quiet and a time to speak up. A time to love and a time to hate. A time for war and a time for peace.

What do people really get for all their hard work? I have thought about this in connection with the various kinds of work God has given people to do. God has made everything beautiful for its own time. He has planted eternity in the human heart, but even so, people cannot see the whole scope of God's work from beginning to end. So, I concluded that there is nothing better for people than to be happy and to enjoy themselves as long as they can. And people should eat and drink and enjoy the fruits of their labor, for these are gifts from God.

I know that whatever God does is final. Nothing can be added to it or taken from it. God's purpose in this is that people should fear him. Whatever exists today and whatever will exist in the future has already existed in the past. (Nothing new under the sun.) For God calls each event back in its turn.

The Injustices of Life

I also noticed that throughout the world there is evil in the courtroom. Yes, even the courts of law are corrupt! I said to myself, "In due season God will judge everyone, both good and bad, for all their deeds."

Then I realized that God allows people to continue in their sinful ways so he can test them. That way, they can see for themselves that they are no better than animals. For humans and animals both breathe the same air, and both die. So, people have no real advantage over the animals. How meaningless! Both go to the same place, the dust from which they came and to which they must return.

For who can prove that the human spirit goes upward, and the spirit of animals goes downward into the earth? So, I saw that there is nothing better for people than to be happy in their work. That is why they are here! No one will bring them back from death to enjoy life in the future.

Every time I read this passage my spirit brings back the memory of when I was a youngster always trying to be a comedian. I learned the hard way that It's not wise to get in grown folks conversations trying to be Mr. Funny (wrong place and wrong time). Mama don't play that. We all better enjoy this life because one day you here and the next day you gone. After this life, then there is judgement. Heaven or hell. Whose side will you be on?

The Suffering Servant
Isaiah 52:13-15 and 53

Isaiah 52–53

Isaiah 53 contains a prophecy of the Atonement of Jesus Christ. Isaiah taught that the Savior would be despised and rejected, smitten and afflicted, that He would carry our sorrows, and that He would be wounded for our transgressions.

By His Stripes We Are Healed

See, my servant will prosper; he will be highly exalted. Many were amazed when they saw him – beaten and bloodied, so disfigured one would scarcely know he was a person. And he will again startle many nations. Kings will stand speechless in his presence. For they will see what they had not previously been told about; they will understand what they had not heard about.

Who has believed our message? To whom, will the Lord reveal his saving power? My servant grew up in the Lord's presence like a tender green shoot, (The term green shoot is a reference to plant growth and recovery). sprouting from a root in dry and sterile ground. There was nothing beautiful or majestic about his appearance, nothing to attract us to him. He was despised and rejected – a man of sorrows, acquainted with bitterest grief. We turned our backs on him and looked the other way when he went by. He was despised, and we did not care.

Yet it was our weaknesses he carried; it was our sorrows that weighed him down. And we thought his troubles were a punishment from God for his own sins. He was beaten that we might have peace. He was whipped, and we were healed! All of us have strayed away like sheep. We have left God's paths to follow our own. Yet the Lord laid on him the guilt and sins of us all.

He was oppressed and treated harshly, yet he never said a word. He was led as a lamb to the slaughter. And as a sheep is silent before the shearers, he did not open his mouth. From prison and trial, they led him away to his death. But who among the people realized that he was dying for their sins – that he was suffering their punishment? He had done no wrong, and he never deceived anyone. But he was buried like a criminal; he was put in a rich man's grave.

But it was the Lord's good plan to crush him and fill him with grief. Yet when his life is made an offering for sin, he will have a multitude of children, many heirs. He will enjoy a long life, and the Lord's plan will prosper in his hands. When he sees all that is accomplished by his anguish, he will be satisfied. And because of what he has experienced, my righteous servant will make it possible for many to be counted righteous, for he will bear all their sins. I will give him the honors of one who is mighty and great, because he exposed himself to death. He was counted among those who were sinners. He bore the sins of many and interceded for sinners.

The most ultimate act of love and kindness. A man without blemish that never committed any sin. We have all strayed away but let's get back to Bible and get connected with God. He deserves all the Glory. Amen

Jesus on the Mountain
Matthew 5-7

Matthew 5–7

The Sermon on the Mount

One day as the crowds were gathering, Jesus went up the mountainside with his disciples and sat down to teach them.

The Beatitudes
This is what he taught them:

God blesses those who realize their need for him, for the Kingdom of Heaven is given to them. God blesses those who mourn, for they will be comforted. God blesses those who are gentle and lowly, for the whole earth will belong to them. God blesses those who are hungry and thirsty for Justice, for they will receive it in full. God blesses those who are merciful, for they will be shown mercy. God blesses those whose hearts are pure, for they will see God. God blesses those who work for peace, for they will be called the children of God. God blesses those who are persecuted because they live for God, for the Kingdom of Heaven is theirs.

God blesses you when you are mocked and persecuted and lied about because you are my followers. Be happy about it! Be very glad! For a great reward awaits you in heaven. And remember, the ancient prophets were persecuted, too.

Teaching about Salt and Light
You are the salt of the earth. But what good is salt if it has lost its flavor? Can you make it useful again? It will be thrown out and trampled underfoot as worthless. You are the light of the world – like a city on a mountain, glowing

in the night for all to see. Don't hide your light under a basket! Instead, put it on a stand and let it shine for all. In the same way, let your good deeds shine out for all to see, so that everyone will praise your heavenly father.

Teaching about the Law
Don't misunderstand why I have come. I did not come to abolish the law of Moses or the writings of the prophets. No, I came to fulfill them. I assure you until heaven and earth disappear, even the smallest detail of God's law will remain until its purpose is achieved. So, if you break the smallest commandment and teach others to do the same, you will be the least in the Kingdom of Heaven. But anyone who obeys God's laws and teaches them will be great in the Kingdom of Heaven. But I warn you – unless you obey God better than the teachers of religious law and the Pharisees do, you can't enter the Kingdom of Heaven at all.

Teaching about Anger
You have heard that the law of Moses says, do not murder. If you commit murder, you are subject to Judgement. But I say, if you are angry with someone, you are subject to Judgement! If you call someone an idiot, you are in danger of being brought before the high council. And if you curse someone, you are in danger of the fires of hell. So, if you are standing before the altar in the Temple, offering a sacrifice to God, and you suddenly remember that someone has something against you, leave your sacrifice there besides the altar. Go and be reconciled to that person. Then come and offer your sacrifice to God. Come to terms quickly with your enemy before it is too late and you are dragged into court, handed over to an officer and thrown in jail. I assure you that you won't be free again until you have paid the last penny.

Teaching about Adultery

You have heard that the law of Moses says, "Do not commit adultery." But I say, anyone who even looks at a woman with lust in his eye has already committed adultery with her in his heart. So, if your eye – even if it is your good eye – causes you to lust, gouge it out and throw it away. It is better for you to lose one part of your body than for your whole body to be thrown into hell! And if your hand – even if it is your stronger hand – causes you to sin, cut it off and throw it away. It is better for you to lose one part of your body than for your whole body to be thrown into hell.

Teaching about Divorce

You have heard that the law of Moses says, "A man can divorce his wife by merely giving her a letter of divorce." But I say that a man who divorces his wife, unless she has been unfaithful, causes her to commit adultery. And anyone who marries a divorced woman commits adultery.

Teaching about Vows

Again, you have heard that the law of Moses says, "Do not break your vows; you must carry out the vows you have made to the Lord! But I say, don't make any vows! If you say, 'By heaven!' it is a sacred vow because heaven is God's throne. And if you say, 'By the earth! it is a sacred vow because the earth is his footstool. And don't swear, 'By Jerusalem!' for Jerusalem is the city of the great King. Don't even swear, 'By my head!' for you can't turn one hair white or black. Just say a simple, 'Yes I will' or 'No, I won't.' Your word is enough. To strengthen your promise with a vow shows that something is wrong.

Teaching about Revenge

You have heard that the law of Moses says, "If an eye is injured, injure the eye of the person who did it. If a tooth gets knocked out, knock out the tooth of the person who did it. But I say, don't resist an evil person! If you are slapped on the right cheek, turn the other, too. If you are ordered to court and your shirt is taken from you, give your coat, too. If a soldier demands that you carry his gear for a mile, carry it two miles. Give to those who ask, and don't turn away from those who want to borrow.

Teaching about Love for Enemies
You have heard that the law of Moses says, "Love your neighbor" and hate your enemy. But I say, love your enemies! Pray for those who persecute you! In that way, you will be acting as true children of your Father in heaven. For he gives his sunlight to both evil and the good, and he sends rain on the just and on the unjust, too. If you love only those who love you, what good is that? Even corrupt tax collectors do that much. If you are kind only to your friends, how are you different from anyone else? Even pagans do that. But you are to be perfect, even as your Father in heaven is perfect.

Teaching about Giving to the Needy
Take care! Don't do your good deeds publicly, to be admired, because then you will lose the reward from your Father in heaven. When you give a gift to someone in need, don't shout about it as the hypocrites do…blowing trumpets in the synagogues and streets to call attention to their acts of charity! I assure you; they have received all the reward they will ever get. But when you give to someone, don't tell your left hand what your right hand is doing. Give your gifts in secret, and your Father, who knows all secrets, will reward you.

Teaching about Prayer and Fasting
And now about prayer. When you pray, don't be like the hypocrites who love to pray publicly on street corners and in the synagogues where everyone can see them. I assure you, that is all the reward they will ever get. But when you

pray, go away by yourself, shut the door behind you, and pray to your Father secretly. Then your Father, who knows all secrets, will reward you.
When you pray, don't babble on and on as people of other religions do. They think their prayers are answered only by repeating their words again and again. Don't be like them, because your Father knows exactly what you need even before you ask him! Pray like this:

The Lord's Prayer
"Our Father in heaven,
May your name be honored.
May your kingdom come soon.
May your will be done here on earth,
Just as it is in heaven.
Give us our food for today,
And forgive us our sins,
Just as we have forgiven those
Who have sinned against us.
And don't let us yield to temptation,
But deliver us from the evil one." (Matthew 6: 9-13)

If you forgive those who sin against you, your heavenly Father will forgive you. But if you refuse to forgive others, your Father will not forgive your sins.
    And when you fast, don't make it obvious, as the hypocrites do, who try to look pale and disheveled so people will admire them for their fasting. I assure you, that is the only reward they will ever get. But when you fast, comb your hair and wash your face. Then no one will suspect you are fasting, except your Father, who knows what you do in secret. And your Father, who knows all secrets will reward you.

Teaching about Money and Possessions

Don't store up treasures here on earth, where they can be eaten by moths and get rusty, and where thieves break in and steal. Store your treasures in heaven, where they will never become moth-eaten or rusty and where they will be safe from thieves. Wherever your treasure is, there your heart and thoughts will also be. Your eye is a lamp for your body. A pure eye lets sunshine into your soul. An evil eye shuts out the light and plunges you into darkness. If the light you think you have is really darkness, how deep that darkness will be.

No one can serve two masters. For you will hate one and love the other or be devoted to one and despise the other. You cannot serve both God and money.

So, I tell you, don't worry about everyday life – whether you have enough food, drink, and clothes. Doesn't life consist of more than food and clothing? Look at the birds. They don't need to plant or harvest or put food in barns because your heavenly Father feeds them. You are far more valuable to him than they are. Can all your worries add a single moment to your life? Of course not.

And why worry about your clothes?

Look at the lilies and how they grow. They don't work or make their clothing, yet Solomon in all his glory was not dressed as beautifully as they are. And if God cares so wonderfully for flowers that are here today and gone tomorrow, won't he more surely care for you? You have so little faith!

So don't worry about having enough food or drink or clothing. Why be like the pagans who are so deeply concerned about these things? Your heavenly Father already knows all your needs, and he will give you all you need from day to day if you live for him and make the Kingdom of God your primary concern.

So don't worry about tomorrow for tomorrow will bring its own worries. Today's trouble is enough for today. Really, no one should be walking around stressed about anything. God has everything under control. God gives us free will, so we must make the decision on who we serve. Who will you serve? If you chose God there are still certain things you must do like humble yourself, pray, seek God's face, turn from your wicked ways, be baptized, and repent for your sins. Make God's kingdom first on your list everyday and watch your life change. God Bless!

Greatest Commandment
Mark 12:28-34

Mark 12

Jesus debated and answered questions when a scribe came along. Jesus answered his question by using Scripture. He emphasized that we must love one another and love God.

The Most Important Commandment

One of the teachers of religious law stood there listening to the discussion. He realized that Jesus had answered well, so he asked, "Of all the commandments, which is the most important?"

Jesus replied, "The most important commandment is this: 'Hear, O Israel! The Lord our God is the one and only Lord.' And you must love the Lord your God will all your heart, all your soul, all your mind, and all your strength! The second is equally important: 'Love your neighbor as yourself!' No other commandment is greater than these."

The teacher of religious law replied, "Well said, Teacher. You have spoken the truth by saying that there is only one God and no other. And I know it is important to love him with all my heart and all my understanding and all my strength, and to offer all of the burnt offerings and sacrifices required in the law. Realizing this man's understanding, Jesus said to him, "You are not far from the Kingdom of God." And after that, no one dared to ask him any more questions.

Parable of the Lost Son
Luke 15:11-32

Luke 15

The main message of the prodigal son is that it doesn't matter how far we stray from our heavenly Father or how much we squander the gifts he provides, he is always delighted when we turn back to him. His unconditional love is waiting for us to return home when he greets us with open arms.

Story of the Lost Son

To illustrate the point further, Jesus told them this story: "A man had two sons. The younger son told his father, 'I want my share of your estate now, instead of waiting until you die.' So, his father agreed to divide his wealth between his sons.

A few days later this younger son packed all his belongings and took a trip to a distant land, and there he wasted all his money on wild living. About the time his money ran out, a great famine swept over the land, and he began to starve. He persuaded a local farmer to hire him to feed his pigs. The boy became so hungry that event he pods he was feeding the pigs looked good to him. But no one gave him anything.

"When he finally came to his senses, he said to himself, 'At home even the hired men have food enough to spare, and here I am, dying of hunger! I will go home to my father and say, "Father, I have sinned against both heaven and you and I am no longer worthy of being called your son. Please take me on as a hired man."'

So, he returned home to his father. And while he was still a long distance away, his father saw him coming. Filled with love and compassion he ran to his son, embraced him, and kissed him.

His son said to him, Father, I have sinned against both heaven and you, and I am no longer worthy of being called your son.

But his father said to the servant, "Quick! Bring the finest robe in the house and put it on him. Get a ring for his finger, and sandals for his feet. And kill the calf we have been fattening in the pen. We must celebrate with a feast, for this son of mine was dead and has now returned to life. He was lost, but now he is found." So the party began.

Meanwhile, the older son was in the fields working. When he returned home, he heard music and dancing in the house, and he asked one of the servants what was going on. Your brother is back, he was told, and your father has killed the calf we were fattening and has prepared a great feast. We are celebrating because of his safe return.

The older brother was angry and wouldn't go in. His father came out and begged him, but he replied, "All these years I've worked hard for you and never once refused to do a single thing you told me to. And in all that time you never gave me even one young goat for a feast with me friends. Yet when this son of yours comes back after squandering your money on prostitutes, you celebrate by killing the finest calf we have.

His father said to him, "Look dear son, you and I are very close, and everything I have is yours. We had to celebrate this happy day. For your brother was dead and has come back to life. He was lost, but now he is found."

Doesn't every family have a member like this? A son, daughter, uncle, or aunt. Someone somewhere has strayed away from the Lord and disobeyed God's commandments. In this evil world (the last days), we need God at all times like never before. Straying away now is not wise. Once you stray away from the Lord, and you continue to commit the same sin (first it becomes a habit, then routine, then the normal way of life), you may lose the divine protection of God by ignoring the Holy Spirit. When you do this, you set yourself up for complete failure. You are open game for all of Satan's lies and deception. Believe this, the devil is not playing with you. He is coming after you with everything he has because he knows his time is running out. That sneaky ol' serpent is trying to get as many people as he can to join his kingdom, but don't fall for his tricks. He wants to turn us away from God and keep us a slave to sin. We must stay connected to God, humble ourselves, pray, and seek God's face daily. All you can really do for someone who has strayed away from the Lord is share the gospel with them, share your testimony with them, and keep them in your prayers. Adults are responsible for their own souls, and one day will stand before God and give accountability for their own lives. Look at it like this, if you willingly give it your all by giving people good advice using wisdom from the Lord to help them get out of whatever sin they are struggling with (porn, drugs, alcohol, etc.) and they disregard it, you have to place it in God's hands and continuously pray for them, and rest assured that God will work it out at his designated time. When they return back, we should celebrate because God is always delighted when we return to the faith, no matter how long we have strayed away.

Eternal Life
John 1:1-18

John I

John's gospel stresses that Jesus Christ was also God. John provides an explanation of his life. He is described in such figurative terms as light, truth, love, good shepherd, the door, the resurrection, the life, living water, bread of life, and more. The beautiful material found in chapters 14-17 reveals the deep love of Jesus for the believers and the peace that comes from faith in him.

Christ, the Eternal World

In the beginning, the Word already existed. He was with God, and he was God. He was in the beginning with God. He created everything there is. Nothing exists that he didn't make. Life itself was in him, and this life gives light to everyone. The light shines through the darkness, and the darkness can never extinguish it.

God sent John the Baptist to tell everyone about the light so that everyone might believe because of his testimony. John himself was not the light, he was only a witness to the light. The one who is the true light, who gives light to everyone was going to come into the world!

But although the world was made through him, the world didn't recognize him when he came. Even in his own land and among his own people, he was not accepted. But to all who believed him and accepted him, he gave the right to become children of God. They are reborn.

This is not a physical birth resulting from human passion or plan – this rebirth comes from God.

So, the Word became human and lived here on earth among us. He was full of unfailing love and faithfulness. And we have seen his glory, the glory of the only Son of the Father.

John pointed him out to the people. He shouted to the crowds, "This is the one I was talking about when I said, 'Someone is coming who is far greater than I am, for he existed long before I did.'"

We have all benefited from the rich blessings he brought to us – one gracious blessing after another. For the law was given through Moses. God's unfailing love and faithfulness came through Jesus Christ. No one has ever seen God. But his only Son, who is himself God, is near to the Father's heart; he has told us about him.

The most important thing to me is that I may have eternal life! What is yours? Is it eternal life, or things of this world?

First, we must have fear of the Lord which is the beginning of understanding. I Love reading the Bible, and listening to various preachers, and their style of preaching. I already have the fear of the Lord, but there is one true man of God that heightens that fear even more. I recommend that if you haven't already, go on social media and search for Pastor Gino Jennings. He is a true Apostle from God. Listen to his messages and get the Word of God. Pastor Jennings teaches about holiness; his church is called First Church of Our Lord Jesus Christ, Inc. based out of Philadelphia, but he has churches located all over the world. Pastor Jennings will teach you the difference between the teaching of God's word, versus a pastor knowing the Scriptures, and just reciting the Bible. One of his sayings is, ("You have to get in there and dissect the Scriptures and make them harmonize.") If we truly want eternal life, we have to be taught the word of God, read the Word of God for ourselves, understand what we have read about the Word of God, pray without ceasing, and apply the Word of God into our daily lives. You should always love thy God with all your heart, mind, body, and soul. God Bless!

The Holy Spirit
John 14:15-27
+ 16:5-15

John 14–16

The Holy Spirit is referred to as the Lord and Giver of Life in the Nicene creed, He is the Creator Spirit, present before the creation of the universe and through his power everything was made in Jesus Christ, by God the Father.

Jesus Promises the Holy Spirit

If you love me, obey my commandments. And I will ask the father, and he will give you another counselor, who will never leave you. He is the Holy Spirit, who leads into all truth. The world at large cannot receive him, because it, isn't looking for him and doesn't recognize him. But you do because he lives with you now and later will be in you. No, I will not abandon you as orphans – I will come to you. In just a little while the world will not see me again, but you will. For I will live again, and you will too. When I am raised to life again, you will know that I am in my Father, and you are in me, and I am in you. Those who obey my commandments are the ones who love me. And because they love me, my Father will love them, and I will love them. And I will reveal myself to each one of them. Jesus said I am the way, the truth, and the life. No one can come to the Father except through me.

The Work of the Holy Spirit

But now I am going away to the one who sent me, and none of you has asked me where I am going. Instead, you are very sad. But it is best for you that I go away, because if I don't, the Counselor won't come. If I do go away, he will come because I will send him to you. And when he comes, he will convince the world of its sin, and God's righteousness, and of the coming judgement. The world's sin is unbelief in me. Righteousness is available because I go to the Father, and you will see me no more. Judgement will come because the prince of this world has already been judged.

Oh, there is so much more I want to tell you, but you can't bear it now. When the spirit of truth comes, he will guide you into all truth. He will not be presenting his own ideas; he will be telling you what he has heard. He will tell you about the future. He will bring me glory by revealing to you whatever he receives from me.

Filled with the Holy Spirit
Acts 2

Acts 2

The book of Acts is a continuation of the Gospel of Luke. Here Luke shows that what Jesus began as a person in earth he continues to do through the Holy Spirit in the life of the church. Acts begins with Jesus' followers being filled with the power of God and preaching so effectively that in one day three thousand people decide to follow Jesus.

The Holy Spirit Comes

On the day of the Pentecost, seven weeks after Jesus' resurrection, the believers were meeting together in one place. Suddenly, there was a sound from heaven like the roaring of a mighty windstorm in the skies above them, and it filled the house where they were meeting. Then, what looked like flames or tongues of fire appeared and settled on each of them. And everyone present was filled with the Holy Spirit and began speaking in other tongues, as the Holy Spirit gave them this ability.

Godly Jews from many nations were living in Jerusalem at that time. When they heard this sound, they came running to see what it was all about, and they were bewildered to hear their own languages being spoken by the believers.

They were beside themselves with wonder. "How can this be?" they exclaimed. "These people are all from Galilee, and yet we hear them speaking the languages of the lands where we were born. Here we are – Parthians, Medes, Elamites, people from Mesopotamia, Judea, Cappadocia, Pontus, the province of Asia, Phrygia, Pamphylia, Egypt, and the areas of Libya toward Cyrene, visitors from Rome (both Jews and converts to Judaism),

Cretans, and Arabians. And we all hear these people speaking in our own languages about the wonderful things God has done. They stood there amazed and perplexed. "What can this mean?" they asked each other. But others, in the crowd were mocking. "They're drunk, that's all!" they said.

Peter Preaches to a Crowd
Then Peter stepped forward with the eleven other apostles and shouted to the crowd, "Listen carefully, all of you fellow Jews and residents of Jerusalem. Make no mistake about this. Some of you are saying these people are drunk. It isn't true. It's much too early for that. People don't get drunk by nine o'clock in the morning. No, what you see this morning was predicted centuries ago by the prophet Joel:

> "In the last days, God said
> I will pour out my spirit
> upon all people.
> Your sons and daughters will
> Prophesy, your young men will
> see visions, and your old.
> Men will dream dreams.
> In those days I will pour out my
> spirit upon all my servants, men
> and women alike, and they will
> prophesy.
> And I will cause wonders in the
> heavens above and signs on the
> earth below – blood and fire and
> clouds of smoke.
> The sun will be turned into darkness,
> and the moon will turn blood red,

before that great and glorious day
of the Lord arrives.
And anyone who calls on the name
of the Lord will be saved."(Acts 2 17-21)

People of Israel, listen. God publicly endorsed Jesus of Nazareth by doing wonderful miracles, wonders, and signs through him, as you well know. But you followed God's prearranged plan. With the help of lawless Gentiles, you nailed him to the cross and murdered him. However, God released him from the horrors of death and raised him back to life again, for death could not keep him in its grip. King David said this about him:

"I know the Lord is always
with me. I will not be shaken,
for he is right beside me.
No wonder my heart is
filled with Joy, and my
mouth shouts his praises!
My body rests in hope.
For you will not leave my soul
among the dead or allow your
Holy One to rot in the grave.
You have shown me the way of life,
and you will give me wonderful Joy
in your presence!"(Acts 2 25-28)

Dear brothers, think about this. David wasn't referring to himself when he spoke these words I have quoted, for he died and was buried, and his tomb is still here among us. But he was a prophet, and he knew God had promised with an oath that one of David's own descendants would sit on David's throne as the Messiah. David was looking into the future and predicting the Messiah's resurrection. He was saying that the Messiah would not be left among the dead and that his body would not rot in the grave.

"This prophecy was speaking of Jesus, whom God raised from the dead, and we all are witnesses of this. Now he sits on the throne of highest honor in heaven, at God's right hand. And the Father, as he has promised, gave him the Holy Spirit to pour out upon us, just as you see and hear today. For David himself never ascended into heaven, yet he said:

> "The Lord said to my Lord,
> Sit in honor at my right hand
> until I humble your enemies,
> making them a footstool under
> your feet."(Acts 2 34-35)

So let it be clearly known by everyone in Israel that God has made this Jesus whom you crucified to be both Lord and Messiah!"

Peter's words convicted them deeply, and they said to him and to the other apostles, "Brothers, what should we do?"

Peter replied, "Each of you must turn from your sins and turn to God and be baptized in the name of Jesus Christ for the forgiveness of your sins. Then you will receive the gift of the Holy Spirit. This promise is to you and to your children, and even to the Gentiles – all who have been called by the Lord our God." Then Peter continued preaching for a long time, strongly urging all his listeners, "Save yourselves from this generation that has gone astray!"

Those who believed what Peter said were baptized and added to the church – about three thousand in all. They joined with the other believers and devoted themselves to the apostles' teaching and fellowship, sharing in the Lord's Supper and in prayer.

The Believer's Meet Together

A deep sense of awe came over them all, and the apostles performed many miraculous signs and wonders. And all the believers met together constantly and shared everything they had. They sold their possessions and shared the proceeds with those in need. They worshiped together at the Temple each day, met in homes for the Lord's Supper, and shared their meals with great joy and generosity – all the while praising God and enjoying the goodwill of all the people. And each day the Lord added to their group those who were being saved. Amen.

Repent I say; and turn from your wicked ways, and sin no more. Have you ever noticed when you're about to do something you know is wrong, a voice inside of you goes off like an alarm? That is the Holy Spirit giving you fair warning. If you go through with this act, afterward you start feeling ashamed and guilty. That is the Holy Spirit convicting you. Trust in the Holy Spirit and you will stay on the straight path.

Salvation
Romans 3

Romans 3

Romans was written by the Apostle Paul. What is salvation? In Christianity, salvation (also called deliverance or redemption) is the "saving [of] human beings from sin and its consequences, which include death and separation from God by Christ's death and resurrection, and the justification following the salvation.

God Remains Faithful

Then what's the advantage of being a Jew? Is there any value in the Jewish ceremony of circumcision? Yes, being a Jew has many advantages. First, the Jews were entrusted with the whole revelation of God.

Some of them were unfaithful, but just because they broke their promises doesn't mean that God will break his promises. Though everyone else in the world is a liar, God is true. As the Scriptures say, "He will be proved right in what he says, and he will win his case in court."

Some say, "our sins serve, a good purpose, for people will see God's goodness when he declared us sinners to be innocent. Isn't it unfair, then, for God to punish us?" (That is the way some people talk.) Of course not. If God is not just, how can God judge and condemn me as a sinner if my dishonesty highlights his truthfulness and brings him more glory? If you follow that kind of thinking, however, you might as well say that the more we sin the better it is. Those who say such things deserve to be condemned, yet some slander me by saying this is what I preach!

All People are Sinners

Well then, are we Jews better than others? No, not at all, for we have already shown that all people, whether Jews or Gentiles, are under the power of sin. As the Scriptures say:

> "No one is good –
> not even one.
> No one has real understanding;
> no one is seeking God.
> All have turned away from God;
> all have gone wrong.
> No one does good.
> not even one."
> "Their talk is foul, like the stench
> from an open grave.
> Their speech is filled with lies."
> "The poison of a deadly snake drips from their lips."
> "Their mouths are full of cursing and bitterness."
> "They are quick to commit murder.
> Wherever they go, destruction and
> misery follow them.
> They do not know what true peace is."
> "They have no fear of God
> to restrain them."(Romans 3 10-18)

Obviously, the law applies to those whom it was given, for its purpose is to keep people from having excuses and to bring the entire world into judgement before God. For no one can ever be made right in God's sight by doing what his law commands. The more we know God's law, the clearer it becomes that we aren't obeying it.

All have sinned and fell short of God's glory.
Avoid God's wrath and believe in Jesus.

Christ Took Our Punishment

God has shown us a different way of being right in his sight – not by obeying the law but by the way promised in the Scriptures long ago. We are made right in God's sight when we trust in Jesus Christ to take away our sins. We all can be saved in this same way no matter who we are or what we have done.

For all have sinned and all fall short of God's glorious standard. Yet God, in his gracious kindness, declared us not guilty. He did this through Christ Jesus who has freed us by taking away our sins. God sent Jesus to take the punishment for our sins and to satisfy God's anger against us. We are made right with God when we believe that Jesus shed his blood and sacrificed his life for us. God was entirely fair and just when he did not punish those who sinned in former times. He is entirely fair and just in this present time when he declares sinners to be right in his sight because they believe in Jesus.

Can we boast, then, that we have done anything to be accepted by God? No, because our acquittal is not based on our good deeds. It is based on our faith. So, we are made right with God through faith and not by obeying the law.

After all, God is not the God of the Jews only, is he? He also the God of the Gentiles. There is only one God, and there is only one way to be accepted by him. He makes people right with himself only by faith, Whether they are Jews or Gentiles. Well then, if we emphasize faith, does this mean that we can forget about the law? Of course not. In fact, only when we have faith can we truly fulfill the law.

Love
1 Corinthians 13

1 Corinthians 13

I have loved you even as the Father has loved me. Remain in my love. When you obey me, you remain in my love just as I obey my Father and remain in his love. I have told you this so that you will be filled with my joy. Yes, your joy will overflow. I command you to love each other in the same way that I love you.

Love is the Greatest

Eagerly desire the greater gifts. Now let me show you the most excellent way.

If I could speak in any language in heaven or on earth but didn't love others, I would only make meaningless noise like a loud gong or a clanging cymbal. If I had the gift of prophecy, and if I knew all the mysteries of the future and knew everything about everything, but didn't love others, what good would I be? If I had the gift of faith so that I could speak to a mountain and make it move but did not have love, I would be no good to anyone. If I gave everything I have to the poor and sacrificed my body, I could boast about it. If I didn't love others, however, I would be of no value whatsoever.

Love is patient and kind. Love is not jealous, boastful, proud, or rude. Love does not demand its own way. Love is not irritable and it keeps no record of when it has been wronged. It is never glad about injustice but rejoices whenever the truth wins out. Love never gives up, never loses faith, is always helpful, and endures through every circumstance.

Love will last forever, but prophecy, speaking in tongues, and special knowledge will all disappear. For even our special knowledge and our prophecy is incomplete. When the end comes, these special gifts will disappear.

When I was a child, I spoke, thought, and reasoned as a child does. When I grew up, I put away childish things. We see things imperfectly, as in a poor mirror, but then we will see everything with perfect clarity. All that I know now is partial and incomplete, but then I will completely know everything just as God knows me.

There are three things that will endure – faith, hope, and love – and the greatest of these is love.

Spiritual Armor
Ephesians 6:10-20

Ephesians 6:10–20

Written by the Apostle Paul. The basic idea in Ephesians is that God's eternal plan is worked out through Christ and his church. When a person believes in Christ, he or she finds new life and safety. God planned this all along and gives everything to believers that they need to live out the Christian life. It is the believer's responsibility, however, to use the resources God provides. Our greatest weakness may be our failure to ask for God's strength.

The Whole Armor of God
Be strong in the Lord's mighty power. Put on all of God's armor so that you will be able to stand firm against all strategies and tricks of the devil. We are not fighting against people made of flesh and blood, but against the evil rulers and authorities of the unseen world, against those mighty powers of darkness who rule this world, and against wicked spirits in the heavenly realms.

Use every piece of God's armor to resist the enemy in the time of evil, so that after the battle you will stand firm. Stand your ground, put on the sturdy belt of truth and the body armor of God's righteousness. For shoes, put on the peace that comes from the good news, so that you will be fully prepared. In every battle you will need faith as your shield to stop the fiery arrows aimed at you by Satan. Put on salvation as your helmet. Take the sword of the spirit, which is the Word of God. Always pray at every occasion in the power of the Holy Spirit. Stay alert and be persistent in your prayers for all Christians everywhere.

And pray for me, too. Ask God to give me the right words as I boldly explain God's secret plan that the good news is for Gentiles, too. I am in chains now for preaching this message as God's ambassador. Pray that I will keep on speaking boldly for him, as I should.

People it's time to wake up and realize the enemy we are up against. Instead, of fighting and killing each other we need to come together and pray one for another. The Bible tells us to be alert, and of a sober mind because your enemy the Devil walks around like a roaring lion seeking out who he may devour. Listen, we must continuously pray for a sound mind. That's how the Devil gets you, by entering your mind, and corrupting your thoughts, and whatever a man thinks he will do. Rebuke all wickedness and pray to the Holy Spirit to give your spirit pure and clean thoughts. Dwell on the things of God and be thankful for his mercy. The Good News is the Devil has already been defeated. Thank you Jesus. May God's grace be upon all who love our Lord Jesus Christ with an undying love.

Right Living
Colossians 3

Colossians 3 was written by Paul the apostle.

Being watchful and alert over your soul and spiritual things is not a cause for doubt over your standing with Christ. It is wisdom for a world of tribulations and dangers to your soul. It is a reminder of the need of prayer and that we are completely dependent upon God.

Living the New Life
Since you have been raised to new life with Christ, set your sights on the realities of heaven, where Christ sits at God's right hand in the place of honor and power. Let heaven fill your thoughts. Do not think only about things down here on earth. For you died when Christ died, and your real life is hidden with Christ in God. When Christ, who is your real life, is revealed to the whole world you will share in his glory.

So put to death the sinful, earthly things lurking within you. Have nothing to do with sexual sin, impurity, or just and shameful desires. Don't be greedy for the good things of this life, for that is idolatry. God's anger will come upon those who do such things. You used to do them when your life was still part of this world. Now is the time to get rid of anger, rage, malicious behavior, slander, and dirty language. Don't lie to each other, for you have stripped off your old evil nature and all its wicked deeds. In its place you have clothed yourselves with a brand new nature that is continually being renewed as you learn more and more about Christ, who created this new nature within you. In this new life, it doesn't matter if you are a Jew or a Gentile, circumcised, barbaric, uncivilized, slave, or free. Christ is all that matters, and he lives in all of us.

Since God chose you to be the holy people he loves, you must clothe yourselves with tenderhearted mercy, kindness, humility, gentleness, and patience. You must make allowances for other's faults and forgive those who offend you. Remember, the Lord forgave you, so you must forgive others. The most important piece of clothing you must wear is love. Love is what binds us all together in perfect harmony. Let the peace that comes from Christ rule in your hearts. As members of one body, you are all called to live in peace. Always be thankful.

Let the words of Christ, in all their richness, live in your hearts and make you wise. Use his words to teach and counsel each other. Sing psalms and hymns and spiritual songs to God with thankful hearts. Whatever you do or say, let it be representative of the Lord Jesus, all the while giving thanks through him to God the Father.

Instructions for Christian Households

Wives must submit to husbands, as is fitting for those who belong to the Lord. Husbands must love their wives and never harshly treat them.

Children must always obey their parents, for this is what pleases the Lord. Fathers don't aggravate your children. If you do, they will become discouraged and quit trying.

Slaves must obey their earthly masters in everything they do. Try to please them all the time not just when they are watching. Obey them willingly because of your reverent fear of the Lord. Work hard and cheerfully at whatever you do, as though you were working for the Lord rather than for people. Remember that the Lord will give you an inheritance as your reward, and the master you are serving is Christ. If you do what is wrong, you will be paid back for the wrong you have done. God has no favorites who can get away with evil.

Words of Wisdom

We can't change the past, and we all must deal with the present, so we might as well get along and prepare for the future. We can't continue to blame one another for our situations. God has a divine plan for everyone, specifically that no man can put asunder. Just do what is right in God's eyes so you can receive your blessings, and get out of any situation you may be in.

Leadership
1 Timothy 3

First Timothy was written by the Apostle Paul near the end of his life. The importance of right belief and right behavior for the theme of this book. Paul stressed that we must know the truth and defend it against the false teachings that will inevitably develop. We must also be very careful to live what we believe so that Satan can't use our own failings against us.

Leaders in the Church

It's true that if someone wants to be an elder desires an honorable responsibility. For an elder must be a man whose life cannot be spoken against. He must be faithful to his wife. He must exhibit self-control, live wisely, and have a good reputation. He must enjoy having guests in his home and must be able to teach. He must not be a heavy drinker or be violent. He must be gentle, peace loving, and not one who loves money. He must manage his family well and have children who respect and obey him. If a man cannot manage his own household, how can he take care of God's church?

An elder must not be a new Christian because he might be proud of being chosen early, and the devil will use that pride to make the man fall. Also, people outside the church must speak well of him so that he will not fall into the devil's trap and be disgraced.

In the same way, deacons must be people who are respected and have integrity. They must not be heavy drinkers and must not be greedy for money. They must be committed to the revealed truths of the Christian faith and live with a clear conscience. Before they are appointed as deacons, they should be given other responsibilities in the church as a test of their character and ability. If they do well, then they may serve as deacons.

In the same way, deacons' wives must be respected and must not speak evil of others. They must experience self-control and be faithful in everything they do.

A deacon must be faithful to his wife, and he must manage his children and household well. Those who do well as deacons will be rewarded with respect from others and will have increased confidence in their faith in Christ Jesus.

The Truths of Our Faith
I am writing these things to you now, even though I hope to be with you soon, so that if I can't come for a while, you will know how people must conduct themselves in the household of God. This is the church of the living God, which is the pillar and support of the truth. Without question, this is the great mystery of our faith.

> Christ appeared in the flesh
> and was shown to be righteous
> by the Spirit.
> He was seen by angels
> and announced to the nations.
> He was believed on in the world
> and was taken up into heaven.

Faith
Hebrews 11

Hebrews is an important letter written to Christians who were perhaps thinking of returning to their old Jewish ways. The author and place are uncertain. The overall superiority of Christ and the Christian life is the central theme of this book. Other religious systems cannot compare with the work that God has done in Christ. Christ is one with God and he did God's work on earth by dying for our sins. What God requires of us now is to trust in him. Through faith, we will receive all that God has for us – now, and in the life to come.

Great Examples of Faith

What is faith? It is the confident assurance that what we hope for is going to happen. It is the evidence of things we cannot yet see. God gave his approval to people in the old days because of their faith.

Through faith, we understand that the entire universe was formed at God's command and that what we see did not come from anything that can be seen.

It was by faith that Abel brought a more acceptable offering to show that he was a righteous man. Although Abel is long dead, he still speaks to us because of his faith.

It was by faith that Enoch was taken up to heaven without dying. "Suddenly he disappeared because God took him." Before he was taken up, he was approved as pleasing to God. So, you see, it is impossible to please God without faith. Anyone who wants to come to God must believe that there is a God and that he rewards those who sincerely seek him.

It was by faith that Noah built an ark to save his family from the flood. He obeyed God, who warned him about something that had never happened before. By his faith he condemned the rest of the world and was made right in God's sight.

It was by faith that Abraham obeyed when God called him to leave home and go to another land that God would give him as his inheritance. Abraham went without knowing where he was going. Even when he reached the land God promised him, he lived there by faith – for he was like a foreigner living in a tent. And so did Isaac and Jacob, to whom God gave the same promise.

Abraham did this because he confidently looked forward to a city with eternal foundations, which was a city designed and built by God.

It was by faith that Sarah, together with Abraham, was able to have a child even though they were too old. Sarah was barren Abraham believed that God would keep his promise. So, a whole nation came from them. Abraham, who was too old to have any children – a nation with so many people that, like the stars of the sky and the sand on the seashore, there is no way to count them.

These faithful people died without receiving what God had promised them, but they saw it all from a distance and welcomed the promises of God. They agreed that they were no more than foreigners and nomads here on Earth. Obviously people who talk like that look forward to a country they can call their own. If they meant the country they came from, they would have found a way to go back. They looked for a better place, a heavenly homeland. That is why God is not ashamed to be called their God, for he prepared a heavenly city for them.

It was by faith that Abraham offered Isaac as a sacrifice when God tested him. Abraham, who received God's promises, was ready to sacrifice Isaac. God had promised him, "Isaac is the son through whom your descendants will be counted." Abraham assumed that if Isaac died, God would bring him back to life again. In a sense, Abraham did receive his son back from the dead.

It was by faith that Isaac blessed his two sons, Jacob and Esau. He had confidence in what God would do in the future.

It was by faith that Jacob, when he was old and dying, blessed each of Joseph's sons and bowed in worship as he leaned on his staff.

It was by faith that Joseph, when he was about to die, confidently spoke of God bringing Israel out of Egypt. He was so sure of it that he commanded them to carry his bones with them when they left.

It was by faith that Moses' parents hid him for three months. They saw that God gave them an unusual child, and they were not afraid of what the King might do.

It was by faith that Moses, when he grew up, refused to be treated as the son of Pharaoh's daughter. He chose to share the oppression of God's people instead of enjoying the fleeting pleasures of sin. He thought it was better to suffer for the sake of the Messiah than to own the treasures of Egypt. He looked ahead to the great reward that God would give him. It was by faith that Moses left the land of Egypt. He was not afraid of the king. Moses kept right on going because he kept his eyes on the one who is invisible. It was by faith that Moses commanded the people of Israel to keep the Passover and to sprinkle blood on the doorposts so that the angel of death would not kill their firstborn sons.

It was by faith that the people of Israel went right through the Red Sea as though they were on dry ground. When the Egyptians followed, they drowned.

It was by faith that the people of Israel marched around Jericho for seven days and the walls crashed down.

It was by faith that Rahab the prostitute did not die with all the others in her city who refused to obey God. She gave a friendly welcome to the spies.

How much more do I need to say? It would take too long to recount the stories of the faith of Gideon, Barak, Samson, Jephthah, David, Samuel, and all the prophets. By faith these people overthrew kingdoms, ruled with justice, and received what God had promised them. They shut the mouths of lions, quenched the flames of fire, and escaped death at the edge of the sword. Their weakness was turned to strength. They became strong in battle and put whole armies to flight. Women received their loved ones back again from death.

Others trusted God and were tortured, preferring to die rather than turn from God and be free. They placed their hope in the resurrection to a better life. Some were mocked, and their backs were cut open with whips. Others were chained in dungeons. Some died by stoning, and some were sawed in half. Others were killed with the sword. Some went about in skins of sheep and goats, hungry, oppressed, and mistreated. They were too good for this world. They wandered over deserts and mountains, and hid in caves and holes in the ground.

All these people mentioned received God's approval because of their faith, yet none of them received all that God promised. God had far better things in mind that would also benefit them, but they can't receive the prize at the end of the race until we finish the race.

Temptation
James 1

James, a brother of Jesus, wrote this around 45-48 A.D. to Christians to provide them with some practical instructions for living. It contains many short, proverbial sayings and reflects Jesus teachings from the Sermon on the Mount. The problems James addressed are pride, discrimination, greed, lust, hypocrisy, meanness, and conformity to an unchristian world. To correct these evils, James illustrates that faith without good deeds is dead (2:26). Merely saying you have certain beliefs is not enough. True faith is seen in a good life.

Greetings from James

This letter is from James, a slave of God and of the Lord Jesus Christ. It is written to Christians scattered among the nations. Greetings.

Faith and Endurance

Dear brothers and sisters, whenever trouble comes your way, let it be an opportunity for joy. For when your faith is tested, your endurance has a chance to grow.

So let it grow, for when your endurance is fully developed, you will be strong in character and ready for anything.

If you need wisdom – if you want to know what God wants you to do – ask him, and he will gladly tell you. He will not resent you asking. When you ask him, be sure that you really expect him to answer, for a doubtful mind is as unsettled as a wave of the sea that is driven and tossed by the wind. People like that should not expect to receive anything from the Lord. They can't make up their minds. They waver back and forth in everything they do.

Christians who are poor should be glad, for God has honored them. And those who are rich should be glad, for God has humbled them. They will fade away like a flower in a field. The hot sun rises and dries up the grass. The flower withers and its beauty fades away. So also, wealthy people will fade away with all their achievements.

God blesses the people who patiently endure testing. Afterward, they will receive the crown of life that God has promised to those who love him. And remember no one who wants to do wrong should ever say, "God is tempting me." God is never tempted to do wrong, and he never tempts anyone else. Temptation comes from the lure of our own evil desires. These evil desires lead to evil actions, and evil actions lead to death. So don't be misled, my dear brothers and sisters.

Whatever is good and perfect comes to us from God above, who created all heaven's lights. Unlike them, he never changes or casts shifting shadows. In his goodness he chose to make us his own children by giving us his true word. And we, out of all creation, became his choice possession.

Listening and Doing

My dear brothers and sisters, be quick to listen, slow to speak, and slow to get angry. Your anger can never make things right in God's sight.

So, get rid of all filth and evil in your lives, and humbly accept the message God has planted in your hearts for it is strong enough to save your souls.

Remember, it is a message to obey, not just to listen to. If you don't obey, you are only fooling yourself. If you just listen and don't obey, it is like looking at your face in a mirror but doing nothing to improve your appearance. You see yourself, walk away, and forget what you look like. If you keep steadily looking into God's perfect law – the law that sets you free – and if you do what it says and don't forget what you heard, then God will bless you for doing it.

If you claim to be religious but don't control your tongue, you are fooling yourself and your religion is worthless. Pure and lasting religion in the sight of God our Father means that we must care for orphans and widows in their troubles and refuse to let the world corrupt us.

Suffering
1 Peter 4

The apostle Peter wrote this letter near the end of his life to comfort and encourage Christians who lived in Asia Minor (now the land of Turkey). He pointed out that suffering was part of the Christian life, and that God would reward those who trusted in him. In case any were thinking of returning to Judaism to escape from persecution, Peter pointed out that Christ's church was God's nation and meant to help others find God (2:9). Peter then presented the example of Christ, who suffered, and urged believers to be prepared for the same experience. Instructions to various groups of Christians end the letter.

The theme of 1 Peter is triumph through suffering. Early Christians lived in difficult times and often paid for their faith with their lives. God knows all that occurs, and his plans for us go beyond our present troubles. We must trust him and live with our eyes lifted to heaven, realizing that our home is there not here on Earth.

This letter is from Peter, an apostle of Jesus Christ. I am writing to God's chosen people who are living as foreigners in the lands of Pontus, Galatia, Cappadocia, the province of Asia, and Bithynia. God the Father chose you long ago, and the Spirit has made you holy. As a result, you have obeyed Jesus Christ and are cleansed by his blood. May you have more and more of God's special favor and wonderful peace.

Living for God

So then, since Christ suffered physical pain, you must arm yourselves with the same attitude he had and be ready to suffer, too. If you are willing to suffer for Christ, you have decided to stop sinning. You won't spend the rest of your life chasing after evil desires, but you will be anxious to do the will of

God. You have had enough in the past of the evil things that godless people enjoy – their immorality and lust, their feasting and drunkenness and wild parties, and their terrible worship of idols.

Of course, your former friends are very surprised when you no longer join them in the wicked things they do, and they say evil things about you. Remember that they will have to face God. He will judge everyone, both the living and dead. That is why the good news was preached even to those who have died – so that although their bodies were punished with death, they could still live in the spirit as God does.

The end of the world is coming soon. Therefore, be earnest and disciplined in your prayers. Most important of all, continue to show deep love for each other, for love covers a multitude of sins. Cheerfully share your home with those who need a meal or a place to stay.

God has given gifts to each of you from his great variety of spiritual gifts. Manage them well so that God's generosity can flow through you. Are you called to be a speaker? Then speak as though God himself were speaking through you. Are you called to help others? Do it with all the strength and energy that God supplies. Then God will be given glory in everything through Jesus Christ. All glory and power belong to him forever and ever. Amen.

Suffering for Being a Christian

Dear friends, don't be surprised at the fiery trails you are going through, as if something strange were happening to you. Instead, be very glad because these trials will make you partners with Christ in his suffering, and afterward you will have the wonderful joy of sharing his glory when it is displayed to all the world.

Be happy if you are insulted for being a Christian, for then the glorious Spirit of God will come upon you. If you suffer, however, it must not be for murder, stealing, making trouble, or prying into other people's affairs.

It is no shame to suffer for being a Christian. Praise God for the privilege of being called by his wonderful name. The time has come for judgement, and it must begin first among God's own children. If we Christians must be judged, what terrible fate awaits those who have never believed God's good news.–

> "If the righteous are barely saved,
> what chance will the godless and
> sinners have?"

So, if you are suffering according to God's will, keep doing what is right and trust yourself to the God who made you, for he will never fail you.

Fellowship!
1 John 1

The Apostle John wrote this letter to believers who were dear to him. He addressed them as his little children and gave them practical instructions for Christian living. He began by stressing that Jesus was God in human form. Those who knew Jesus knew God the Father as well. Those who did not know Jesus did not know God, nor did they know God's love. Christians, however, have experienced the love of God in their lives and have no need to fear – either in this life or in life after death.

John stressed the basic truths of the Christian faith to comfort and encourage those whom he called his children in the faith. His message of love, forgiveness, being in a community, dealing with sin, and living as holy people brought God's light to a dark world.

Introduction

The one who existed from the beginning is the one we have heard and seen. We saw him with our own eyes and touched him with our own hands. He is Jesus Christ, the word of life. The one who is life from God was shown to us, and we have seen him. Now we testify and announce to you that he is the one who is eternal life. He was with the Father, and then he was shown to us. We are telling you about what we ourselves have seen and heard, so that you may have fellowship with us. And our fellowship is with the Father and with his Son, Jesus Christ.

We are writing these things so that our joy will be complete.

Living in the Light

This is the message he has given us to announce to you. God is light and there is no darkness in him at all. So we are lying if we say we have fellowship with God but go on living in spiritual darkness. We are not living in the truth. If we live in the light of God's presence, just as Christ is, then we have fellowship with each other, and the blood of Jesus, his Son, cleanses us from every sin.

If we say we have no sin, we are only fooling ourselves and refusing to accept the truth. If we confess our sins to him, he is faithful and just to forgive us and to cleanse us from every wrong. If we claim we have not sinned, we call God a liar and show that his word has no place in our heart.

Heaven
Revelation 21-22

The glorious book of Revelation shows the once humiliated Jesus, the Lamb of God, slain for the sins of the world, as he takes control of history at the end of times and brings eternal good to pass by destroying evil and establishing holy power forever and ever. It is Christians' hope that someday all will be well, and we will live with God. Tears shall be wiped away, and death, sorrow, crying, and pain shall be gone forever (21:4)

The New Jerusalem

Then I saw a new heaven and a new Earth, for the old heaven and the old earth had disappeared. And the sea was also gone. And I saw the holy city, the new Jerusalem, coming down from God out of heaven like a beautiful bride prepared for her husband. I heard a loud shout from the throne, saying, "Look, the home of God is now among his people! He will live with them, and they will be his people. God himself will be with them. He will remove all of their sorrows, and there will be no more death or sorrow or crying or pain for the old world and its evils are gone forever."

And the one sitting on the throne said, "Look, I am making all things new!" And then he said to me, "Write this down for what I tell you is trustworthy and true." And he also said, "It is finished! I am the Alpha and the Omega – the Beginning and the End. To all who are thirsty I will give the springs of the water of life without charge! All who are victorious will inherit all these blessings, and I will be their God, and they will be my children. But cowards who turn away from me, and unbelievers, and the corrupt, and murders, and the immoral, and those who practice witchcraft, and idol worshipers, and all liars – their doom is in the lake that burns with fire and sulfur, this is the second death."

Then one of the seven angels who held the seven bowls containing the seven last plagues came and said to me, "Come with me! I will show you the bride, the wife of the Lamb."

So, he took me in spirit to a great, high mountain, and he showed me the holy city, Jerusalem, descending out of heaven from God. It was filled with the glory of God and sparkled like a precious gem, crystal clear like Jasper. Its walls were broad and high, with twelve gates guarded by twelve angels. And the names of the twelve tribes of Israel were written on the gates. There were three gates on each side – east, north, south, and west. The wall of the city had twelve foundation stones, and on them were written the names of the twelve apostles of the Lamb.

The angel who talked to me held in his hand a gold measuring stick to measure the city, its gates, and its wall. When he measured it, he found it was a square, as wide as it was long. In fact, it was in the form of a cube, for its length and width and height were each 1,400 miles. Then he measured the walls and found them to be 216 feet thick (the angel used a standard human measure).

The wall was made of Jasper, and the city was pure gold, as clear as glass. The wall of the city was built on foundation stones inlaid with twelve gems; the first was Jasper, the second sapphire, the third agate, the fourth emerald, the fifth onyx, the sixth carnelian, the seventh chrysolite, the eighth beryl, the ninth topaz, the tenth chrysoprase, the eleventh jacinth, the twelfth amethyst.

The twelve gates were made of pearls – each gate from a single pearl. And the main street was pure gold, as clear as glass.

No temple could be seen in the city, for the Lord God Almighty and the Lamb are its temple. And the city has no need of sun or moon, for the glory of God illuminates the city, and the Lamb is its light. The nations of the earth will walk in its light, and the rulers of the world will come and bring their glory to it. Its gates never close at the end of day because there is no night. And all the nations will bring their glory and honor into the city. Nothing evil will be allowed to enter – no one who practices shameful idolatry and dishonesty – but only those whose names are written in the Lamb's Book of Life.

And the angel showed me a pure river with the water of life, clear as crystal, flowing from the throne of God and of the Lamb, coursing down the center of the main street. On each side of the river grew a tree of life, bearing twelve crops of fruit, with a fresh crop each month. The leaves were used for medicine to heal the nations.

No longer will anything be cursed, for the throne of God and of the Lamb will be there, and his servants will worship him. And they will see his face, and his name will be written on their foreheads. And there will be no night there – no need for lamps or sun – for the Lord God will shine on them. And they will reign forever and ever.

Then the angel said to me, "These words are trustworthy and true: 'The Lord God, who tells his prophets what the future holds, has sent his angel to tell you what will happen soon.'"

Jesus is Coming

"Look, I am coming soon! Blessed are those who obey the prophecy written in this scroll."

I, John, am the one who saw and heard all these things. And when I saw and heard these things, I fell down to worship the angel who showed them to me. But again, he said, "No, don't worship me. I am a servant of God, just like you and your brothers the prophets, as well as all who obey what is written in this scroll. Worship God!"

Then he instructed me, "Do not seal up the prophetic words you have written, for the time is near. Let the one who is doing wrong continue to do wrong; the one who is vile, continue to be vile; the one who is good, continue to do good; and the one who is holy, continue in holiness."

"See, I am coming soon and my reward is with me, to repay all according to their deeds. I am the Alpha and the Omega, the First and the Last, the Beginning and the End."

Blessed are those who wash their robes so they can enter through the gates of the city and eat the fruit from the tree of life. Outside the city are the dogs – the sorcerers, the sexually immoral, the murderers, the idol worshipers, and all who love to live a lie.

"I, Jesus have sent my angel to give you this message for the churches. I am both the Source of David and the heir to his throne. I am the bright morning star."

The Spirit and the bride say, "Come." Let each one who hears them say, "Come." Let the thirsty ones come – anyone who wants to. Let them come and drink the water of life without charge. And I solemnly declare to everyone who hears the prophetic words of this book: If anyone adds anything to what is written here, God will add to that person the plagues described in this book. And if anyone removes any of the words of this prophetic book, God will remove that person's share in the tree of life and in the holy city that are described in this book.

He who is the faithful witness to all these things says, "Yes, I am coming soon!" Amen! Come, Lord Jesus!

The grace of the Lord Jesus be with you all.

I have truly been blessed, and I want this book to shine as my light even after I'm long gone. Always live your life by putting God first, and let no man put asunder what God has in store for your destiny. Proverbs 3: 5-6 states, "Trust in the Lord with all thine heart and lean not unto thine own understanding. In all thy ways acknowledge him and he shall direct thy paths." God bless.

www.ingramcontent.com/pod-product-compliance
Lightning Source LLC
LaVergne TN
LVHW010318281224
799994LV00036B/172